SEARCH THE ZOO
FIND THE ANIMALS

Bethanie and Josh Hestermann
Illustrated by Sara Lynn Cramb

ROCKRIDGE
PRESS

In loving memory of Hilda Tresz —B.H. and J.H.

*To my husband, Justin, for his limitless support and encouragement,
and to all of the amazing animals that live on this planet,
I am constantly awed and inspired by you —S.L.C.*

First Rockridge Press hardcover edition 2022

Originally published in trade paperback by Rockridge Press 2020

Rockridge Press and the Rockridge Press logo are trademarks or registered trademarks of Callisto Media Inc. and/or its affiliates in the United States and other countries and may not be used without written permission.

For general information on our other products and services, please contact our Customer Care Department within the United States at (866) 744-2665, or outside the United States at (510) 253-0500.

Hardcover ISBN: 979-8-88608-669-0
Paperback ISBN: 978-1-64876-128-7

Manufactured in the United States of America

Interior and Cover Designer: Stephanie Sumulong
Art Producer: Michael Hardgrove
Editor: Laura Bryn Sisson
Production Editor: Jenna Dutton

Custom Illustration © 2020 Sara Lynn Cramb

Author Photo: Genevieve Elaine Photography
Illustrator Photo: Justin Cramb

10 9 8 7 6 5 4 3 2 1 0

Contents

WELCOME TO THE ZOO

Exploring the zoo is a great way to see animals up close. This lets you learn about them in a whole new way! Sometimes zoo animals are tricky to spot, but that's part of the fun.

You will meet wonderful animals from all around the world right here in this book. On each page, read about the animals and other things hidden in the picture, then try to find them. For even more fun, search for the extras, too.

Some animals in zoos are **endangered**. Zoos help people learn about these animals and what they face in the wild. Zoos also teach people how they can help protect the animals and places they love. When you're done visiting this zoo, you will know how you can help, too.

Ready to come on in? Welcome to the zoo!

THINGS TO FIND

Peacock

Stuffed Animal

Popcorn

Pigeon

Zookeeper

Fountain

Zoo Map

Chocolate Ice-Cream Cone

Reusable Cup

Ball Python

WHERE'S THE PEACOCK?

Peacocks use their feathers to show off. Females are called pea*hens*! The peacock roams all over the zoo. Search for him on every page.

5

AFRICAN SAFARI

If you visit Africa, you may be lucky enough to see elephants, lions, giraffes, rhinos, and zebras living in open, grassy areas called savannas. You can see many of these animals in the African Safari **exhibit** at the zoo. What do you think you will find?

ANIMALS OF AFRICA

Zebra
Are zebras black with white stripes or white with black stripes? The answer is black with white stripes! Zebras eat grass and live within reach of watering holes where they can drink.

African Buffalo
Adult African buffalos have thick, curved horns. A male's horns connect in the middle of its forehead to form a bony shield called a boss.

Lion

Lions are sometimes called "kings of the jungle," even though they don't live in the jungle. Lions hunt animals like wildebeests and zebras but spend most of each day resting and sleeping.

Giraffe

A giraffe's long neck, legs, and tongue help it reach leaves way up in tall trees. Unlike lions, giraffes sleep for only minutes at a time—less than half an hour per day.

Ostrich

An ostrich can be almost nine feet tall and is the largest bird on Earth. It can't fly, but it can run really fast. Ostriches have just two toes on each foot.

Rhinoceros

Rhinoceros means "nose horn." Can you see why? Rhinos have thick, gray skin and large, strong bodies. They like getting muddy. Mud helps keep rhinos cool and protects their skin from bugs.

MORE TO FIND ON THE SAVANNA

Warthog

Secretary Bird

Spotted Hyena

African Wild Dog

THE WATERING HOLE

Watering holes are gathering places on the African savanna. Thirsty animals, both big and small, come from all over to drink at the same place.

7

THE GREEN HEART OF AFRICA

You've learned about the African savanna where lions and giraffes roam. There are also deserts in Africa, like the mighty Sahara Desert. But the middle of Africa is green. Gorillas, pygmy hippos, and many more animals live their hidden lives in the forests and swamplands of Africa.

WHAT TO FIND IN THE FOREST

Gorilla
Gorillas are smart, powerful animals that eat fruit, roots, and even tree bark. Adult male gorillas are called silverbacks because their backs have a patch of silver hair.

Mandrill
Mandrills are monkeys with bright red and blue faces, yellow beards, and colorful backsides. They have pouches in their cheeks for storing food, like chipmunks!

Okapi

Its backside may have zebra stripes, but okapis (oh-COP-ees) are related to giraffes. Okapis have long, black tongues and oily, chocolate-colored fur that's as soft as velvet.

Pygmy Hippo

Pygmy hippos are a kind of small hippopotamus. They're shiny because their skin oozes fluid that helps protect them from the sun . . . just like sunscreen!

Blue Duiker

A blue duiker (DIE-ker) is brown or gray with a blue tint. Its tail is dark on the top and white on the bottom. These little antelopes flick their tails to communicate with each other.

Crowned Eagle

Crowned eagles are **predators**. These forest birds hunt and eat animals like monkeys and duikers. The feathers around their heads look like crowns.

SECRETS OF THE AFRICAN FOREST

Bongo

Shoebill

African Gray Parrot

Chimpanzee

A TALE OF APES AND MONKEY TAILS

Gorillas, chimpanzees, and orangutans are apes, not monkeys. Here's an easy way to tell: Most monkeys have tails, but apes do not.

WILD AUSTRALIA

Australia is famous for its Outback, a large, wild area in the middle of the country made mostly of hot, dry desert and grassland **habitats**. Few people live there, but many animals do. Australia also has woodlands and rainforests.

Red Kangaroo

Red kangaroos can grow six feet tall and travel 25 feet in a single leap. Kangaroos can also go 30 miles per hour by hopping on their back legs. How fast can *you* hop?

Koala

Like kangaroo moms, koala moms have pouches where their babies stay for about six months after birth. Koalas live in trees and eat leaves that are **poisonous** to most animals.

Tasmanian Devil

Tasmanian devils have a strong bite and will eat just about anything. They have mostly black fur with a couple of white patches. In the wild, Tasmanian devils live on the Australian island of Tasmania.

Short-Beaked Echidna

Echidnas (eck-ID-nas) have sharp spines called quills, long, thin snouts, and even longer tongues for catching insects. They have no teeth. Unlike other **mammals**, echidnas lay eggs.

Red-Necked Wallaby

Can you find what looks like a small kangaroo? It's a wallaby! Red-necked wallabies have long feet, tails, and ears. They live in Australia's forests and woodlands.

Tawny Frogmouth

A tawny frogmouth is not an owl, but it sure looks like one. It's hard to spot this insect-eating bird because its feathers look just like a tree branch.

IN AND AROUND THE OUTBACK

Laughing Kookaburra

Thorny Devil Lizard

Ringtail Possum

Dingo

UNIQUE, DANGEROUS AUSTRALIA

Many animals are found *only* in Australia, and nowhere else. Australia is also home to some of the most dangerous snakes in the world.

JOURNEY THROUGH ASIA

Central Asia has mountains, forests, and grassy plains called steppes. As you explore this exhibit, you may spot a camel on the steppe, a giant panda in the bamboo forest, and even a snow leopard on the rocks. Can you find a markhor (goat) with twisty horns?

WONDERS OF CENTRAL ASIA

Red Panda
The red panda has red fur, a white face, and a striped tail like a raccoon's. To keep warm in the cold mountains, red pandas wrap themselves in their big bushy tails.

Snow Leopard
This shy cat has white fur and dark spots—perfect **camouflage** in the snowy mountains. Snow leopards make a "chuffing" sound instead of roaring. Their large paws keep them from sinking into the snow.

Japanese Macaque

Known as snow monkeys, red-faced Japanese macaques (muh-KAKS) live farther north than any other monkeys on Earth. They like to play with stones by stacking them and knocking them down.

Golden Takin

A golden takin's fur keeps it warm in the mountains. Oily skin helps it stay dry in the rain and mist. Takins are related to sheep.

Giant Panda

A giant panda spends half of every day eating, and its favorite meal is bamboo. Adult pandas are black and white, but baby pandas are born pink with some white hairs.

Moon Bear

A moon bear has shaggy black fur with a light V-shaped mark on its chest. It climbs trees in its forest habitat. Sometimes, it walks on two legs like a human!

EXTRA CREDIT

Golden Snub-nosed Monkey

Saker Falcon

Pallas's Cat

Bactrian Camel

ALL ABOUT BAMBOO

Bamboos are giant grasses that can grow almost three feet in one day! There are hundreds of types of bamboo in China, where pandas live.

TROPICAL ASIA

Tropical places tend to be warm, wet, and full of life. Some of the most amazing animals on the planet—like elephants, tigers, and Komodo dragons (the largest lizards on Earth)—roam, hunt, and live in the tropical forests of Southeast Asia.

ASIAN ANIMALS OF THE TROPICS

Orangutan

Orangutans build nests in the treetops, where they rest and sleep. Their arms are long and strong—perfect for climbing trees. Orangutans have red-brown fur that grows long and looks shaggy.

Asian Elephant

Elephants are the largest animals on land. They also have large brains, large ears to help keep them cool, and very strong trunks. There are no bones in an elephant's trunk, just muscles.

Tiger

Tigers can be even bigger than lions! Unlike lions, tigers tend to live alone, except for tiger moms with cubs. And unlike most other cats, tigers like to swim.

Malayan Tapir

A Malayan tapir (TAY-per) looks like a black-and-white pig with an elephant's trunk, but it's neither pig nor elephant. Tapirs' front feet have four toes and their back feet have three.

Komodo Dragon

The Komodo dragon is one of Earth's top predators, but it only lives on a few islands in Southeast Asia. This large, **venomous** lizard flicks its long tongue to "smell" the air.

Binturong

Do you smell popcorn? It's probably the binturong, which looks like a bear mixed with a cat. Binturongs have dark fur, whiskers, and a long tail that can grab branches. And they smell like popcorn!

MORE IN THE TROPICS

Rhinoceros Hornbill

Raggiana Bird of Paradise

Asian Small-Clawed Otter

Siamang

ELEPHANTS OF THE WORLD

Asian elephants are smaller than the elephants on the African savanna, and their ears are rounder. A third type of elephant, the forest elephant, also lives in Africa and is the smallest of the three.

CREATURES OF THE NIGHT

As the sun goes down, the day begins for nocturnal animals. They sleep while it's light outside and are active while it's dark. You can visit nocturnal animals from all over the world in the Creatures of the Night exhibit . . . *if* you can find them!

IN THE DEN OF DARKNESS

Aye-Aye
Tap, tap, tap. Who's there? It's an aye-aye, using its extra-long middle finger to tap the tree trunk in search of insects to eat. Aye-ayes have yellow eyes, big ears, and skinny fingers.

Aardvark
Aardvarks have long noses, kind of like pig snouts, and claws for digging. Aardvarks sleep in underground burrows during the day and come out at night to dig for insects.

Crested Porcupine

Sharp quills cover a crested porcupine's body. Some quills can be a foot long! When faced with a predator, a porcupine's quills stick up, making it look big and scary.

Pygmy Slow Loris

The first thing you'll notice about this little animal is its big, round eyes that help it see without much light. Pygmy slow lorises are cute, but their bite can be **toxic**.

Vampire Bat

Vampire bats sleep upside-down during the day with their wings wrapped around them like blankets. They drink blood from sleeping animals like cows, pigs, and horses, but the sleeping animals usually don't even notice.

Naked Mole Rat

Since naked mole rats live under-ground, these pink, wrinkled animals live in darkness all the time. They have small eyes and use their large teeth for digging.

NIGHT CRAWLERS

Tokay Gecko

Great Horned Owl

Hedgehog

Striped Skunk

WORDS TO KNOW

Nocturnal means being active at night. Diurnal (die-ER-nul) means being active during the day. Are you nocturnal or diurnal?

MADAGASCAR

There's nowhere in the world quite like Madagascar, a large island off the coast of Africa in the Indian Ocean. Some animals, like lemurs, only live on Madagascar! The island has dry forest habitats, rainforests, and deserts. Take a peek inside this fun exhibit.

MADE IN MADAGASCAR

Sifaka Lemur
Sifaka lemurs leap from tree to tree using their powerful back legs. On the ground, sifakas hop sideways on two legs. They have white fur with dark red patches.

Hedgehog Tenrec
Short spines cover most of a hedgehog tenrec's small body. It rolls into a little ball to protect itself from predators.

Panther Chameleon

A chameleon can look right and left at the same time by moving its eyes in different directions! Its sticky tongue is as long as its body.

Fossa

The top predator on Madagascar, the fossa, hunts lemurs. Fossas have brown fur and look like cats with round ears. They use scent to communicate with each other.

Baobab Tree

Baobabs are strange-looking trees that store water in their thick trunks. They grow in Africa, Madagascar, and Australia. Baobab trees provide food and shelter for many animals.

Flying Fox

A flying fox is a bat that mostly eats fruit. A bat's wings are actually its hands! Bats have four finger-like bones in each wing.

BONUS FIND

Tomato Frog

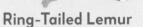

Ring-Tailed Lemur

Madagascar Day Gecko

Crested Coua

WHY DO CHAMELEONS CHANGE COLORS?

Do chameleons change colors for camouflage? Not really. They change colors based on their moods and to communicate with other chameleons.

REPTILE HOUSE

Tortoises, iguanas, and crocodiles—what do these animals have in common? They're all reptiles. Reptiles have scales or bony plates (or both) covering their bodies, they are **cold-blooded**, and most of them lay eggs. Have fun exploring the Reptile House!

Nile Crocodile

That's no log—it's a crocodile. Nile crocodiles can be 14 feet long or more. Crocs are great parents. They make nests and guard their eggs until they hatch.

Emerald Tree Boa

The green emerald tree boa is a constricting snake—it squeezes its **prey**. This boa gives birth to live babies that are not green, but orange or red.

20

Galápagos Tortoise

This giant tortoise can live more than 100 years! Its life is pretty great. It eats cactus and other plants, basks in the sun, and takes long naps.

Gila Monster

This venomous "monster" has bumpy black and orange (or black and pale pink) skin. It stores fat in its tail. If it needs to, it can go months without eating.

Green Iguana

An iguana can drop its tail to confuse predators and then often regrows it later. Green iguanas can be six or more feet long. They're great swimmers.

King Cobra

A king cobra's bite is deadly. This big snake looks even bigger when it flexes its neck muscles to show off its "hood." King cobras are often nine to 12 feet long.

REPTILES

IN THE REPTILE HOUSE

Savannah Monitor

Chinese Giant Salamander

Pig-Nosed Turtle

Dwarf Caiman

"CROC" OR "GATOR"

Crocodiles have V-shaped snouts, while alligators have U-shaped snouts. If top *and* bottom teeth poke out of its closed mouth, it's a croc.

AMAZING AMAZON

South America is home to the largest rainforest on Earth, the Amazon. A rainforest has warm temperatures and lots of rain. About one in every 10 **species** on Earth lives there. That's a lot of plants and animals!

Golden Lion Tamarin

Picture a monkey with a lion's mane and you have a golden lion tamarin. Golden lion tamarins have red-gold fur and usually give birth to twins.

Two-Toed Sloth

Two-toed sloths spend almost their whole lives in trees. They have long, curved claws to help them hang on to branches upside-down. Sloths move really, really slowly.

Toucan

You can't miss this tropical bird's brightly colored beak. That long beak helps a toucan reach fruit on faraway branches, and it may also help keep the bird cool.

Giant Anteater

The giant anteater is built for eating thousands of ants every day! It uses its long tongue and sticky spit to catch its tiny prey.

Jaguar

Jaguars are big cats that live in the Americas. Rosettes, the dark spots on a jaguar's coat, help camouflage a jaguar in the rainforest.

Kinkajou

A kinkajou lives in trees. Using its skinny tongue, it drinks nectar from flowers and honey from beehives. By **pollinating** flowers, kinkajous help the rainforest grow.

HIDDEN IN THE RAINFOREST

Ring-Tailed Coati

Squirrel Monkey

Poison Dart Frog

Giant River Otter

AMAZON RUBBER TREES

Rubber starts out as milky liquid oozing from a tree— a rubber tree! Rubber trees grow in South American rainforests.

SNOW FOREST

As you travel north in North America, snow forests turn into cold, treeless plains called the Arctic tundra. Animals in chilly places have special traits called adaptations, like warm fur coats or the ability to sleep through the winter. Learn more in the Snow Forest exhibit.

A LOOK INSIDE THE SNOW FOREST

Grizzly Bear
A grizzly bear gets ready for winter by eating lots of food and digging a den where it will sleep through the cold months. Female grizzlies wake up to give birth.

Caribou
A caribou's antlers fall off and grow back each year. A caribou has two coats of fur on its body to help it stay warm. Fur even covers its nose!

Gray Wolf

A gray wolf stays warm while sleeping by wrapping its tail around its face. Wolves live and hunt in groups called packs. Dogs bark, but wolves howl. (*Ah-oooooo!*)

Canada Lynx

Big, furry paws and webbed toes help a Canada lynx walk, run, and hunt on the snow. The bigger an animal's paws, the less it sinks in fluffy snow.

Snowy Owl

A snowy owl's eyes are so big it can hardly move them. Owls must turn their heads to see. Their heads can turn almost all the way around.

Bald Eagle

Bald eagles spot prey (usually fish), then swoop down and grab it with sharp claws called talons. A bald eagle's nest can be huge, almost 10 feet across!

NORTHERN NOTABLES

American Mink

Arctic Fox

Bison

Canada Goose

WINTER IN THE NORTH

Some animals **hibernate** through long, cold winters, while bears and other animals go into a light hibernation or "winter sleep." Others travel south until it warms up. *Brr!*

LIFE ON THE FARM

Animals and humans have lived and worked together for a very long time. Pets and farm animals that live with humans—like goats, sheep, and pigs—are called domesticated. You'll see these animals in the Life on the Farm exhibit.

African Pygmy Goat
Goats are curious and social. They like to climb and jump, just like human kids. Young goats are even called kids!

Donkey
Donkeys look like short horses with floppy ears. Male donkeys are called jacks, and female donkeys are jennies. Donkeys groom each other, just like monkeys.

Sheep

Check out your pupils (those black circles in your eyes) in a mirror. A sheep's eyes are different—they have horizontal (side-to-side) pupils shaped like rectangles.

Pig

Pigs are smart. They have short legs and large bodies that weigh up to 700 pounds. To keep cool, pigs take mud baths.

Llama

Llamas have long necks and are related to camels. Llamas spit at other llamas to say, "I'm in charge here."

Cow

As a cow eats, it chews just enough to swallow. After some rest, it coughs the food (called cud) back up and chews it again.

MORE FRIENDLY FACES

Rooster

Axis Deer

Duck

Rabbit

BABIES ON THE FARM

A baby goat is a "kid," a baby llama is a "cria," and a baby goose is a "gosling."

COASTAL LIVING

There's a whole world to discover along the coast. Some animals, like penguins, seabirds, and sea lions, spend part of their time on land and part at sea. Others spend their whole lives just offshore in the ocean.

CREATURES OF THE COAST

Humboldt Penguin

Not all penguins live in cold places. Humboldt penguins are warm-weather penguins. They nest on coasts and hunt for fish in the ocean.

Brown Pelican

A brown pelican dives into the ocean and scoops fish-filled seawater into its throat pouch. It tips its head to drain the water before swallowing the fish.

Sea Lion

Sea lions like to lie in the sun, then hunt for squid and fish in the ocean. Their whiskers can sense movement in the water.

Giant Pacific Octopus

A giant Pacific octopus has eight arms covered with suckers that help it taste and smell. An octopus squirts a cloud of ink at predators to help it escape.

Inca Tern

Inca terns are black seabirds with funny white mustaches. Their beaks and feet are red or orange.

Sea Otter

Sea otters have a lot of fur—up to one million hairs per inch of their bodies! This thick fur keeps their skin dry even as they swim underwater.

HIDE-AND-SEEK BY THE SEA

Harbor Seal

Cownose Ray

Crested Auklet

Horned Puffin

ENRICHMENT FOR ZOO ANIMALS

Zoo animals love to play! You will see toys, feeder balls (balls with food hidden inside), and other types of **enrichment** in animals' exhibits.

DESERTS OF THE WORLD

A desert is a place that doesn't get a lot of rain. These dry places are often hot, but sometimes a desert is cold, like Antarctica (the South Pole). In hot deserts, animals have to get creative to stay cool and find food and water.

DESERT DWELLERS

Fennec Fox
Giant ears help a fennec fox keep cool in the heat and listen for insects underground. This cute fox's sand-colored fur matches the desert sand.

Meerkat
Can you find the meerkat, a fuzzy little animal standing on its back legs? Meerkats are good diggers. They live in tunnels that can be more than six feet underground.

Turkey Vulture

Vultures are scavengers—they eat dead things. Scavengers help keep **ecosystems** healthy. Turkey vultures have bald heads and a great sense of smell, and they hiss!

Arabian Oryx

When you spot a pair of long, straight horns, you've found the Arabian oryx. Its light fur helps keep it cool under the desert sun.

Dromedary Camel

What's in that hump? A camel's hump stores fat—a lot of fat! There are two types of camel. A dromedary has one hump and a Bactrian camel has two.

Burrowing Owl

Don't look for burrowing owls in a tree! They live in burrows on the ground, eating grasshoppers and other bugs.

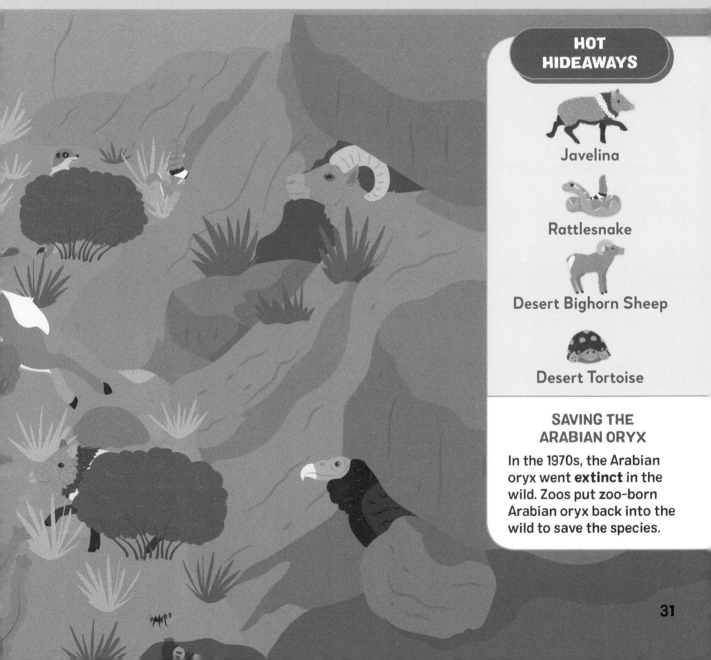

HOT HIDEAWAYS

Javelina

Rattlesnake

Desert Bighorn Sheep

Desert Tortoise

SAVING THE ARABIAN ORYX

In the 1970s, the Arabian oryx went **extinct** in the wild. Zoos put zoo-born Arabian oryx back into the wild to save the species.

31

BUG HOUSE

The Bug House is the perfect place to learn about bugs, insects, spiders, and other creepy-crawly critters. Most insects have **exoskeletons**, wings, six legs, and two antennae on top of their heads. They live nearly everywhere on Earth. Many creepy-crawly critters are very helpful to humans.

BEST OF THE BUG HOUSE

Leaf Insect

One of these leaves is not like the others. One is a leaf insect! To look even more like a real leaf, a leaf insect may sway in the wind.

Praying Mantis

A praying mantis is green and sticklike, with a triangle-shaped head. In a flash, it snatches its prey with its long, spiky front legs.

Emperor Scorpion

What's black and has eight eyes, two pincers, and a curved tail with a venomous stinger? An emperor scorpion!

Hercules Beetle

A Hercules beetle can be seven inches long, if you include its horn. Male Hercules beetles use their horns to battle each other.

Rose-Haired Tarantula

Rose-haired tarantulas are hairy, venomous spiders with fangs. They eat insects, frogs, and mice. Tarantulas throw sharp hairs from their bodies to scare away predators.

Monarch Butterfly

The beautiful monarch butterfly is black, orange, and white. Butterflies taste with their feet. They use their long tongues like straws to slurp nectar from plants.

MORE COOL CRITTERS

Banana Slug

Walking Stick

Domino Roach

Black Widow

HOW INSECTS BREATHE

Insects don't breathe like humans and many other animals do, because they don't have lungs. Instead, insects breathe through their skin.

CONSERVATION STATION

Thank you for visiting the zoo! Now that you've learned about some of the animals that call Planet Earth home, you may wonder what you can do to help them.

When we take care of the earth, we take care of the animals that live here—including ourselves! You and your family can help take care of our planet by making some small changes. Use less water by taking shorter showers and keeping the faucet off while you brush your teeth. Try not to use plastic bags and straws, and try not to buy food with palm oil in it. (Keep reading to learn why.)

SAVE THESE SPECIES

Rhinoceros
Rhinos are in trouble. Some people hunt rhinos because they use their horns to make things other people buy. Hunting endangered animals is called poaching.

Orangutan
Many things at the grocery store have palm oil in them. Orangutans are endangered because humans cut down their forest homes to make palm oil.

Aye-Aye
In Madagascar, some people are afraid of aye-ayes. They think aye-ayes will bring them bad luck, so if they see one, they get rid of it.

Elephant
Poaching affects elephants, too, because some people want their tusks. Elephants in the wild also struggle because humans compete with them for space.

Polar Bear
Human activities are warming the earth, melting large sheets of sea ice where polar bears hunt. Without sea ice, it is hard for polar bears to hunt for food.

Koala
Humans cut down trees to make space for things like homes and farms. But when we cut down too many trees, animals like koalas lose their homes.

THE FINAL ROUND

Gorilla

Giant Panda

Tasmanian Devil

Golden Lion Tamarin

Answer Key

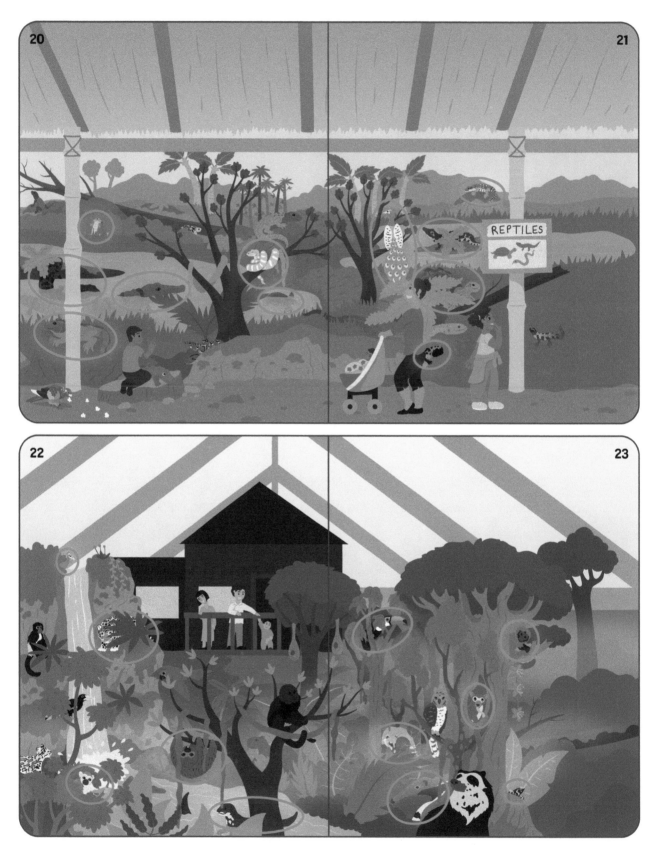

28

29

30

31

42

Glossary

camouflage: The ability to blend in by matching the background

cold-blooded: Animals whose body temperatures change with the temperature of the air or water around them

ecosystem: A community of plants and animals living together

endangered: At risk of going extinct and disappearing from the wild

enrichment: Things (objects or even other animals) added to an animal's living space to make its life better

exhibit: The place an animal lives at a zoo or aquarium

exoskeleton: A skeleton on the outside of an animal's body

extinct: A plant or animal that has disappeared from the wild

habitat: The place an animal lives

hibernate: Going into a really deep sleep during the cold winter months (bears go into a lighter sleep called winter sleep)

mammal: An animal that has a backbone and hair or fur, can keep its body warm (warm-blooded), and in most cases gives birth to live babies

poisonous: Something that can be harmful if touched or eaten

pollinating: Bringing pollen from one plant to another plant, which can help create new plants

predator: An animal that eats other animals for food

prey: An animal that other animals eat for food

species: A group of the same kind of animal

toxic: Harmful, sometimes poisonous

venomous: An animal that uses a harmful substance called venom to injure other animals, usually by bite or sting

About the Authors

Bethanie and Josh Hestermann are authors of animal-science books for kids. They wrote *Search the Ocean, Find the Animals*, as well as *Zoology for Kids* and *Marine Science for Kids* for advanced readers (ages 9+). Bethanie is a freelance writer, and Josh is a zoologist working at the California Science Center. They live in Southern California with their two kids.

About the Illustrator

Sara Lynn Cramb illustrates educational books for kids. She has created illustrations for many titles, including *Search the Ocean*, *Find the Animals*, *Animals of the World: A Lift-the-Flap Book*, and *Out and About: Night Explorer*. Sara loves creating work that excites and educates kids about the natural world.

CPSIA information can be obtained
at www.ICGtesting.com
Printed in the USA
JSHW041642030622
26676JS00001B/3